The Chri

Jazz
Preludes
Collection

Christopher Norton (signature)

BOOSEY & HAWKES

CHRISTOPHER NORTON

Christopher Norton was born in New Zealand in 1953. After graduating he began his career as a teacher, pianist and composer, and began to develop an interest in popular music. Coming to the UK in 1977 on a university scholarship, he studied composition at York University with Wilfred Mellers and David Blake. Well established as a composer, producer, arranger and educationalist, Norton has written stage musicals, ballet scores, piano music, popular songs and orchestral music as well as jingles and signature tunes for TV and radio. He has lectured all over the world on aspects of his work and likes to integrate traditional teaching methods with aspects of modern technology.

Chris is best known for his world-famous series *Microjazz* — easy graded pieces in modern styles such as blues, rock 'n' roll, reggae and jazz — and for his award-winning *Essential Guides* to Pop Styles, Latin Styles and Jazz Styles. He has also created the *Micromusicals* series – short curriculum-linked musicals for children aged 5-11.

www.christophernorton.com

IAIN FARRINGTON

Iain Farrington has an exceptionally busy and diverse career as a pianist, organist, composer and arranger. He studied at the Royal Academy of Music, London and at Cambridge University. He has made numerous recordings, and has broadcast on BBC Television, Classic FM and BBC Radio 3.

As a solo pianist, accompanist, chamber musician and organist, Iain has performed at all the major UK venues. Abroad he has given concerts in the USA, Japan, South Africa, Malaysia, China and all across Europe. He has worked with many of the country's leading musicians, including Bryn Terfel, Sir Paul McCartney and Lesley Garrett. Iain played the piano at the opening ceremony of the London 2012 Olympics with Rowan Atkinson, the London Symphony Orchestra and Sir Simon Rattle. He regularly performs with ensembles including the London Sinfonietta and the Britten Sinfonia, as well as all the major London orchestras.

www.iainfarrington.com

Published by Boosey & Hawkes Music Publishers Ltd
Aldwych House
71–91 Aldwych
London
WC2B 4HN

www.boosey.com

ISMN 979-0-060-13934-5
ISBN 978-1-78454-736-3

First published 2006
This impression 2023

Printed by Halstan:
Halstan UK, 2-10 Plantation Road, Amersham, Bucks, HP6 6HJ. United Kingdom
Halstan DE, Weißliliengasse 4, 55116 Mainz. Germany

Cover design by Chloë Alexander Design

Solo piano performances performed by Iain Farrington
Band audio production by Frank Mizen for CN Productions

Cover images:
Oleg Afonin, "Street jazz in Russia_VII" | September 11, 2015 via Flickr, Creative Commons Attribution.
Maxime Auger, "Jazz man" | July 13, 2014 via Flickr, Creative Commons Attribution.
esbie, "club de jazz" | January 15, 2008 via Flickr, Creative Commons Attribution.
Miles Heller, "Jazz Elements #5" | March 23, 2011 via Flickr, Creative Commons Attribution.
Maria Eklind, "Jazz" June 13, 2015 via Flickr, Creative Commons Attribution.

The Christopher Norton

Jazz Preludes

Collection

AUDIO RESOURCES

Stream or download audio for this book via the web address below or scan the QR code.

https://**audio.boosey.com/R22F**

Up and away

Christopher Norton

 Up and Away is written in a ragtime style with a chacteristic stride piano pattern in the left hand. An easygoing and syncopated main theme in D major is contrasted with a more *legato* section that moves further away from the main key.

Tie break

Christopher Norton

This blues piece has a grinding 5th–6th–b7th pattern in the left hand which provides an anchor for the increasingly restless improvisation–like phrases in the right hand.

Jazz fantasy

Christopher Norton

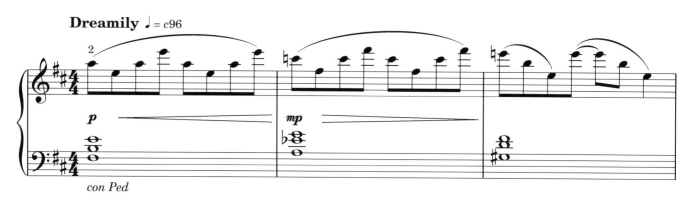

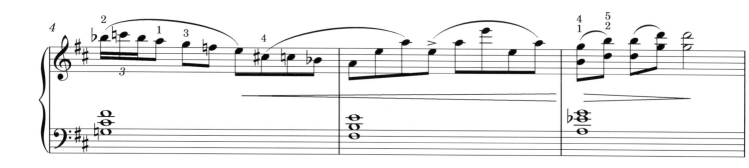

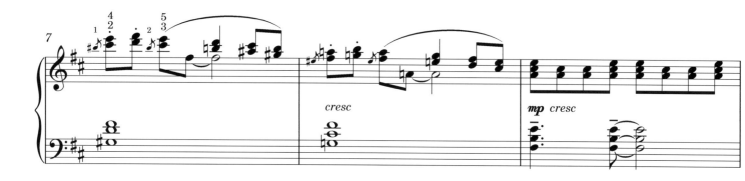

 Jazz Fantasy is a dreamy, impressionistic piece with rootless left hand chords providing a warm and mysterious chordal backdrop for predominantly arpeggiated right hand figures. It is formed of one long melody.

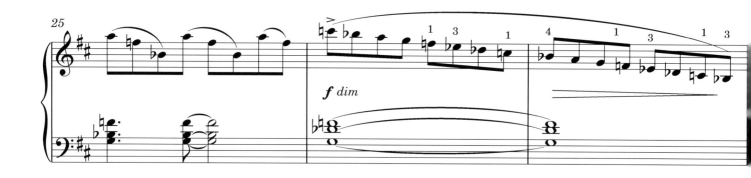

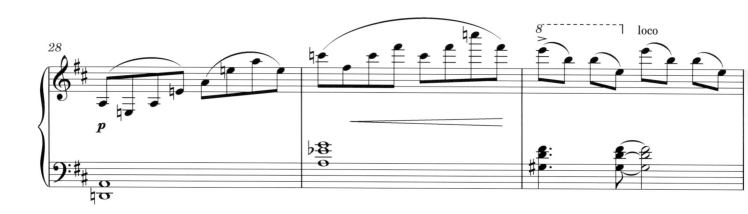

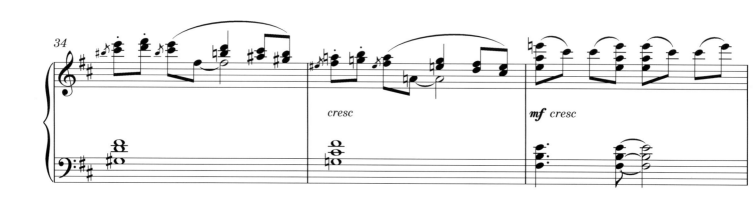

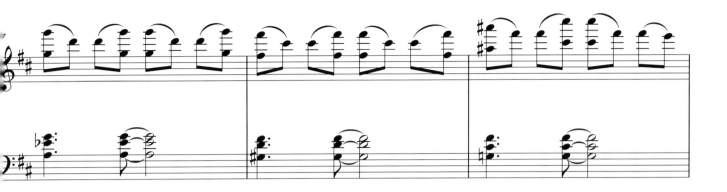

Sparkling

Christopher Norton

This extroverted swing piece has a bright repeated theme that is followed by a more mellow response. A restatement of the main theme leads to an improvisation-like section which becomes brassy and declamatory, then delicate and fleet-fingered.

Tough love

Christopher Norton

 Starting quietly but rhythmically, this piece builds in intensity, and contains with a complex improvisation-like section in the centre. The left hand stacked fourth voicings have their roots in Miles Davis' modal masterpiece, *Kind of Blue* – as well as in the work of Herbie Hancock.

Blue April

Christopher Norton

Blue April is an intense jazz ballad, requiring *rubato* and a beautiful sound. The plaintive main melody is played in various registers and grows organically so that the piece feels like one extended melody.

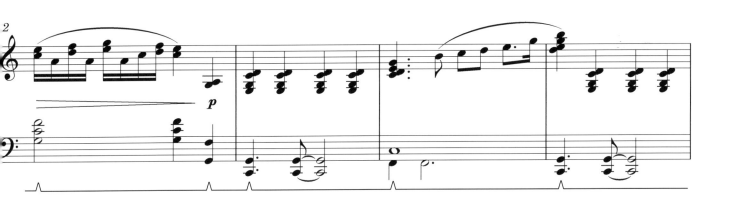

much slower

Beech Street

Christopher Norton

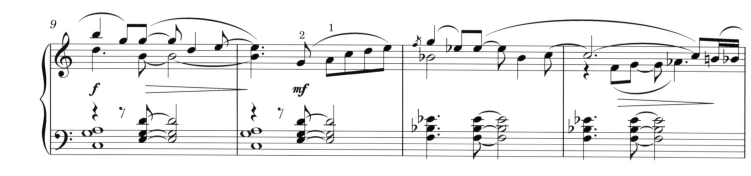

 Beech Street is written in a 'cool' jazz style, with left hand chords in fourths providing accompaniment to a modally-inflected right hand melody. The main theme is contrasted with a gently rhythmic Latin figure that returns several times in varied forms.

[Blank]

Without you

Christopher Norton

 Another plaintive jazz ballad, *Without You* unfolds in relaxed paragraphs, with a second idea emerging and flowering to a brief climax before a quiet restatement of the main theme.

New kid

Christopher Norton

 The opening of this traditional swing style piece has a Charleston flavour. An improvisation-like section builds to a dramatic and impressive-sounding 'locked hand' passage. Whimsical in style, the piece seems to be ending gently but then goes out with a bang!

The moonlit sky

Christopher Norton

 In a gentle swing style, this jazz ballad has an emulation of a 4-in-a-bar jazz guitar strumming in the left hand part whilst the right hand plays an expressive syncopated melody. The piece later develops into a more complex piece harmonically, with rich chords played by both hands and explorations of chords quite far removed from the initial C major.

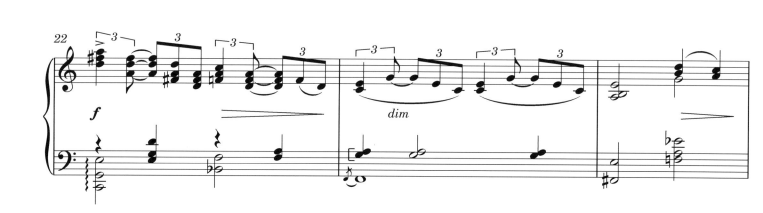

Chicken feed

Christopher Norton

This is the most extroverted and fastest-moving piece in the collection. A thrusting main theme in fourths winds its way to a bluesy figure, underpinned by rootless left hand chords. A statement up an octave ushers in a gradual build up and a James Brown style all-out gospel workout. The main theme returns, and the piece draws to a close with a raucous and punchy ending.

Latinate

Christopher Norton

With intensity ♩ = 156

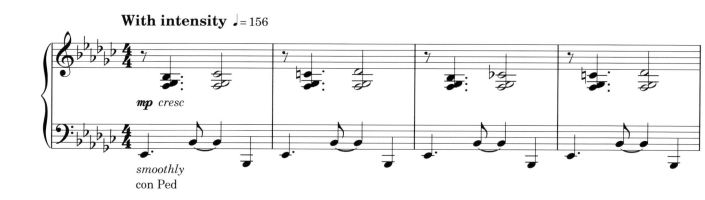

The opening chordal section builds inexorably to a Latin-influenced rhythmic figure and a sinuous main theme, which is somewhat Spanish in flavour. These ideas are all stirred about and toyed with resulting in a very restless feel.

The still night

Christopher Norton

A ¾ ballad, *The Still Night* has rich chords underpinning an expressive melody, full of intricate figures and kaleidoscopic chord changes. A rising chromatic figure near the end is particularly striking and the piece uses the same figure to disappear mysteriously into silence.

Rollicking

Christopher Norton

With a stride piano left hand accompaniment, the right hand plays an extroverted and syncopated melody that is full of slightly surprising twists and turns. The momentum is retained from beginning to end.

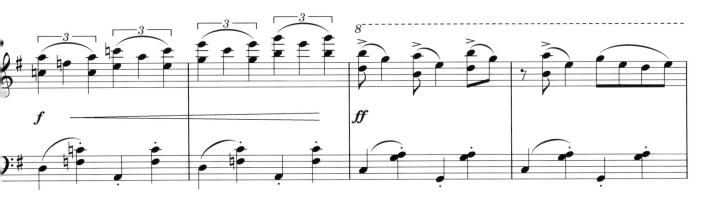

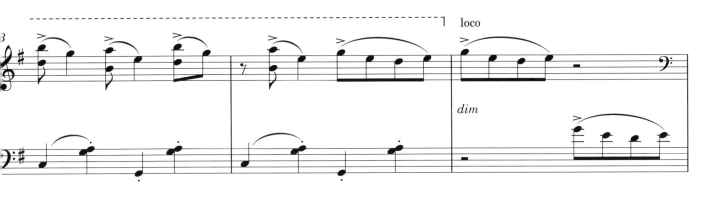